Wheels Around Renfrewshire

by
Robert Grieves

Bridge of Weir railway viaduct *c.*1920. A Manson 4-4-0 'Greenock Bogie' in its dark green livery hauls a train of late-Victorian coaches from the station and heads towards Kilmacolm, next stop down the Glasgow & South Western Railway's line towards its terminus at Greenock (Princes Pier). James Manson was locomotive superintendent of the G&SWR from 1890 until 1912, during which time he designed and produced no less than fifteen classes of railway engine. The section of track from Kilmacolm to Greenock closed to passenger traffic in 1966, and was cut back further in 1983 when Bridge of Weir and Kilmacolm stations were closed, thus ending their rail link to Glasgow. Today the weir on the River Gryffe seen in this view is also gone, as are the tannery buildings to the right.

© Robert Grieves, 2004.
First published in the United Kingdom, 2004,
by Stenlake Publishing
Telephone: 01290 551122
Printed by Cordfall Ltd, Glasgow, G21 2QA

ISBN 1 84033 274 3

The publishers regret that they cannot supply
copies of any pictures featured in this book.

Waters' scrapyard at Linwood Toll was a well-known local eyesore for many years, being clearly visible to all passing traffic on the main road between Paisley and Johnstone. After lengthy discussions and prevarications the yard closed and the motor mountain was cleared c.1965. Visible among the many examples of what had once been the pride and joy of their owners are various models of Ford, Hillman, Morris, Rover, Vauxhall and Volkswagen. The tracked Jones crane with its latticed jib which moved the cars around the premises was undoubtedly the hardest-worked vehicle in the yard, and may be seen in the foreground.

FOREWORD

I have spent much of my working life as a bus and coach driver, and was employed by several companies in Renfrewshire including Cunningham of Paisley, Graham of Hawkhead, McGill of Barrhead, Paton of Renfrew and Western SMT (later Clydeside Buses) at Paisley, Inchinnan and Thornliebank depots. All these firms are, of course, now only memories, and it is memories which form the basis of the majority of the scenes in the 'Wheels' series, of which this is the thirteenth title to be published.

Since my schooldays in Paisley I have collected as a hobby photographs of long-forgotten transport scenes around Scotland, and these are brought to you in the pages of this family of books. The majority are of early bus and coach travel because of my predominant interest in these areas, but wherever possible are complemented by other forms of wheeled transport.

Wheels Around Renfrewshire takes readers on a journey back over the years to revisit some of the former transport interest in the county. Regionalisation took place in 1975 and Renfrewshire then became a district within the newly created Strathclyde Region, although for the purposes of this book the relevant area is taken to be that delineated by the old county boundaries.

I would like to thank all those who have assisted with additional information and photographs for this book, including the late James Anderson, Tom Blair, Alan Brotchie, Alan Linklater (Malcolm Group), Ian Maclean, W. A. C. Smith, Ian Taylor and Jim Thomson.

This photograph was taken in 1969 of myself at the wheel of a Guy Arab in the fleet of McGill of Barrhead. This bus started life in April 1944 (as I did!) when wartime specifications were Spartan. It was originally fitted with what was known as a 'utility' type body, built by Park Royal of London, and had wooden slatted seats instead of upholstered ones. Regulations were eased at the end of hostilities and in 1955 CHS 254 received replacement bodywork by Massey Bros. of Wigan, as seen here.

From 1890 John Currie of Kilbarchan provided a horse bus service between the village and Milliken Park railway station, offering a connection with trains for Paisley and Glasgow. In 1905, however, he withdrew the service due to a drop in custom caused by competition from the recently opened Kilbarchan station. Had he remained in business, he would have met even stiffer opposition from the Paisley District Tramway Co. which extended the tram service from Johnstone to the village in 1906. This illustration from late Victorian times shows Currie's two-horse brake outside Barr's grocery store at Kilbarchan Cross, with some of the local 'Habbies' in attendance. Note the thatch-roofed building behind the worthies. Kilbarchan station, built by the Glasgow & South Western Railway on its Dalry and North Johnstone loop line, closed to passengers in 1966, and much of the former trackbed is now a cycle track.

Cross Arthurlie Street, Barrhead, seen in September 1910 as the local water cart passes Campbell's shop, dampening the dusty roadway with a water sprinkler fed from the large barrel above. Most local authorities continued to use water carts throughout the Edwardian period, some of which were hired from private owners, although in this instance the cart belonged to the Burgh of Barrhead. Approaching in the opposite direction, towards T. A. Ewing's drapery store, is another horse-drawn cart, this one owned by a local dairyman. During the school summer holidays the water cart was a major attraction for local children who would splash along barefoot behind it, enjoying the fun but usually the wrath of the horseman.

Horse-drawn charabanc excursions were very popular in the late nineteenth and early twentieth century. Naturally, when motor vehicles increased in numbers from the early 1900s onwards, the number of horse-drawn wagons decreased. Some, such as this one owned by carriage hirers and funeral directors P. B. Wright of Greenock, managed to survive later than others. This view in Brougham Street was captured outside the town's King's Theatre in the late 1920s, shortly after it had been renamed (initially having been the Alexandra, built in 1905). In its original form the Alexandra had been a rather lavish venue for touring drama and opera companies and when it reopened as the King's it was advertised as 'Greenock's premier talkie house'. The jolly group aboard the three-horse charabanc were members of the cast of the Frances Letty show, performing at the King's at the time, and were perhaps off for a jaunt to Lunderston Bay, which was always a popular picnic spot for trips from Greenock. The theatre was acquired by the Rank organisation in the mid-1950s and reopened as the Odeon. Eventual closure took place in 1969 and the fine building was demolished in 1973 as part of Greenock's road-widening programme.

Long before it became fashionable to lead a healthy lifestyle, Johnstone man Dugald Semple left his employment as an engineering draughtsman to enjoy the simple life in the open air. In August 1907 he pitched his tent on Linwood Moss, but when winter approached more comfort was required and Dugald purchased a second-hand horse-drawn bus (minus horses) which had plied on the streets of Glasgow. This he converted to his main living quarters on the Moss, transporting it to his next location when he moved to Goldenlea, about a mile from Bridge of Weir. He lived happily on this site for the next ten years, broken by a couple of years in London where he lectured on food economy as a pacifist during the First World War. This picture shows Dugald at Bridge of Weir with the old bus, which he appropriately named 'Wheelhouse'. Also visible is his bell tent and possibly a tasty pot of soup simmering above the fire. Dugald was what would now be described as a vegan, using neither milk, eggs nor even honey in his cooking. He later moved to a croft near Beith in neighbouring Ayrshire where he took up fruit farming, but continued to write and lecture on healthy living. His books included *Life in the Open*, *Living in Liberty* and *Joys of the Simple Life*.

This photograph was taken at Houston point-to-point races in the mid-1920s and shows members of the Young family enjoying a grandstand view from the vantage point of one of their old horse-drawn coaches. Some of those included in the picture are: James Leckie Young (the boss), with bowler and binoculars (left of centre); a teenage Ian Young in the front row with cap; while on the very top is William Gordon Young (Ian's brother and known as Gordon). The Youngs were amongst the best-known transport families in Scotland, having started as carriage hirers and funeral undertakers in Paisley in the 1880s. A regular service of horse buses was inaugurated in 1886 between County Square and Colinslee, followed soon after by a service to Meikleriggs. A fifteen-minute service was provided on the former route until 1905, but with the arrival of electric trams opposition proved overwhelming and the horse bus service was discontinued. The Meikleriggs service did not suffer from tramway competition and survived until 1914. In 1925 the first of what was to become the largest fleet of motor buses in Renfrewshire – and the biggest privately-owned fleet in Scotland – was operated between Glasgow, Paisley and Johnstone, and later to Largs and to West Kilbride.

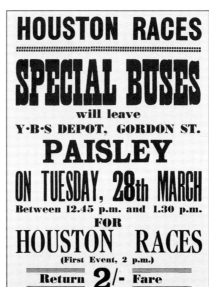

HOUSTON RACES
SPECIAL BUSES
will leave
Y·B·S DEPOT, GORDON ST.
PAISLEY
ON TUESDAY, 28th MARCH
Between 12.45 p.m. and 1.30 p.m.
FOR
HOUSTON RACES
(First Event, 2 p.m.)

Return **2/-** Fare

NOW BOOKING   Telephone: PAISLEY 3191
YOUNGS' BUS SERVICE LTD.

Young's Colinslee horse bus in the 1890s. The drivers of these vehicles were well-known Paisley worthies and each had a nickname. For instance, John Lockie, the regular Colinslee driver, was 'Rosy Morn', while jovial Jimmy Wallace of the Meikleriggs bus was 'Yellow Tail'.

An advertising poster for Young's special buses from Paisley to the Houston races in 1939.

7

HS 38 was a 12 h.p. Arrol–Johnston 30 cwt. delivery lorry built at Underwood in Paisley and registered in February 1904 to Alexander Kennedy's Castlebank Laundry of Anniesland. It should be remembered that part of Renfrew Parish extended to include this area on the north bank of the River Clyde. In 1912 Anniesland, Jordanhill and Scotstoun East were transferred to Glasgow, but it was not until 1926 that Scotstoun West and Yoker came under the city's control. This explains why many motors based in those areas bore the Renfrewshire HS registration letters, and also why vehicle manufacturers such as Albion of Scotstoun and Halley of Yoker taxed many of their products in Renfrewshire. The Castlebank Laundry (listed in early directories as Castlebank Steam Carpet Beating Works) originated in the 1870s in Castlebank Street, Partick, moving to roomier premises near Anniesland Cross in the 1890s as the business boomed. The company's fleet of canary yellow delivery lorries was well-known throughout Central Scotland, as was their advertising slogan – 'Mother, here comes the Castlebank man' – sign-written on every member of the fleet. Yellow must have been Alex Kennedy's favourite colour since in 1904 his private car (HS 66) was a Panhard 7 h.p. tonneau painted the same shade as his lorries. To modern eyes the appearance of the lumbering solid-tyred vehicle seen above with its chain drive and acetylene lamps can only be described as primitive. However, a century ago the heavy load of hampers full of laundry from various Castlebank agencies in the Glasgow area could be collected and delivered more quickly and cheaply using this lorry than by horse-drawn transport.

Motor vehicle licensing was introduced to Renfrewshire (along with most other local authorities throughout the British Isles) in December 1903. HS was the registration mark allocated to the county, whereas VS was issued to the Burgh of Greenock and XS to Paisley. Several of the most prominent gentlemen in the county naturally wished to have the first numbers to be issued, and shipowner William Lithgow of Drums, Langbank, received HS 1 for his 5 h.p. Daimler phaeton. He also owned HS 2, a 12 h.p. Wolseley tonneau, while HS 3 was a Paisley-built 12 h.p. Arrol–Johnston dogcart owned by Robert Drummond of Lylesland Terrace, Paisley (Drummond was the road surveyor for Renfrewshire County Council). Archibald Campbell, Lord Blythswood of Blythswood House, Renfrew (pictured on page 14), registered a Daimler 7 h.p. wagonette as HS 22. This picture shows HS 9, which was allocated to an Albion A3 type 12 h.p. car owned by Robert Paton of Cartbank, Johnstone, who was one of the partners in the Johnstone mills which specialised in the production of shoelaces and linen thread. HS numbers reached 9999 in June 1937, after which the sequence moved progressively through the alphabet from AHS to YHS until the system of suffix letters commenced with AHS . . . B in March 1964. As is still common practice today, certain registration allocations went to those who simply wished their initials. For example, Harry Smith of imposing-sounding Albemarle Mansions, London, received HS 81 for his motorcycle in 1905, and the following number was also specially requested since HS 82 went to Major Henri Samuel of Carlisle Castle for his Argyll tonneau.

Andersons of Newton Mearns was a well-known name in motoring circles throughout Scotland. Starting in Victorian times as coal merchants and contractors, the family business had enlarged by the advent of the twentieth century to include a Humber cycle agency, which was soon followed by an interest in the newfangled motor car, then in its infancy. It was perhaps a natural progression to obtain a dealership in Humber motor cars, a relationship which was to last through that company's lifetime and subsequently through the years of the Rootes Group. This picture, taken outside Andersons premises in Kilmarnock (Ayr) Road, Newton Mearns, shows brothers Robert and James Anderson in the front seat of an 8½ h.p. Humber car, registered HS 39 in March 1904. Records show that the car was finished in a shade of carmine red and that this number was transferred within a few months to a 10 h.p. Humber, also registered to Robert Anderson. Andersons Garage in Newton Mearns closed in 1980 and the former site is now covered by the Asda supermarket.

The first petrol station in Renfrewshire was built at Thornliebank by Andersons of Newton Mearns in the mid-1920s. It was situated where Stewarton Road meets Paisley Road – a spot known locally as the 'Jenny Lind' after an inn of the same name on the original site, named after the nineteenth century soprano known as the 'Swedish nightingale'. The car at the pumps (which dispensed Shell and Benzole brands) was an Armstrong–Siddeley 'Four 14' fabric saloon. This flat-radiator model was the last before the famous pre-select gearbox was introduced. The photograph dates from around 1928 and today the roundabout at the Thornliebank / Stewarton / Paisley Road junction is adjacent to where the scene was photographed. The Anderson family were pioneers of the car trade in Renfrewshire once the motor age dawned at the turn of the twentieth century.

Below: Renfrewshire could boast several motor manufacturers in Edwardian days. Prominent were Albion Motors of Scotstoun and Halley Motors of Yoker, remembering that the county extended over to the north side of the Clyde at that time. In Paisley the Arrol–Johnston company had its factory in Underwood, where the 24/30 h.p. landaulette shown here was built around 1908. Arrol–Johnston produced a good-quality, reliable car which was popular throughout Britain, and this particular example was owned locally by Dr Donald Crerar, a well-known dentist in Renfrew. Taken from 'Dunard', his home and surgery, the photograph looks up the main Paisley road towards Moorpark. The street to the right is Albert Road and the scene is virtually unchanged today.

In 1909 Arrol–Johnston introduced this style of car with 'coal scuttle' bonnet, a design also favoured by Renault at the time. The cars were thoroughly tested prior to delivery, and these scenes show a 15.9 h.p. model in chassis form being put through its paces by Mr Reid, the company's chief tester, over rough terrain on Paisley's Gleniffer Braes in 1912. The following year the company moved production from Paisley to Dumfries.

Familiar wheels around Renfrew belonged to this 1922 Morris Cowley 'Bullnose', registered V 9969. It ran in the town for over half a century and was thus very well-known to local folk, as was its owner, Joan Gilchrist of Newmains Farm, seen here at the wheel. Joan – a kenspeckle figure in her beret – would deliver milk from the Cowley and carry bales of hay or even farm animals in it. When asked, as she often was, why she didn't buy a new car, her reply was inevitably 'Ye canny carry cauves in the back o' a new caur wi' a roof'. Newmains Farm, where this view was taken, was at the top end of Newmains Road where the prefabs adjacent to Renfrew Aerodrome may be seen. Also in this scene from 1960 are Joan's elderly sisters Jenny and Aggie, along with Archie McCulloch, a well-known Scottish TV personality of the period, whose Jag is also visible. When Joan was no longer physically able to drive her old Cowley, it passed to myself for renovation and preservation, and still attends motoring events (although no longer carrying calves!) under new ownership.

Most of us must have drunk the distinctive-tasting Camp Coffee at some time, and it is one of those beverages you either love or loathe. In mid-Victorian times Robert Paterson & Sons, originators of the brand, were described as manufacturing chemists, with premises in King Street and Osborne Street, Glasgow, where they produced 'sauces, table jellies, vinegar, pickles and fruit wines'. The development of Camp Coffee came in the 1870s, and although a bottled essence of coffee and chicory it quickly achieved popularity as the world's first instant coffee brand. Business expansion resulted in a move to new factory premises in Charlotte Street near Glasgow Green, and the business remained there until it closed in the 1980s. The family home was near Clarkston, Renfrewshire, and this scene from 1913 shows Robert Paterson, boss of the business at that time, with his wife and daughters in HS 560, their new chauffeur-driven dark green Humber 14 h.p. tourer. The picture was posed with Robert Paterson at the wheel, and not the chauffeur, who appears somewhat confused and is looking away from the camera, unlike the family. At the top of the driveway is the Paterson residence, Stamperland House. Camp Coffee is still available today, but the manufacturing rights are now owned by food giant McCormick Europe. It is produced in East Lane, Paisley, once the home of Smith's potato crisps.

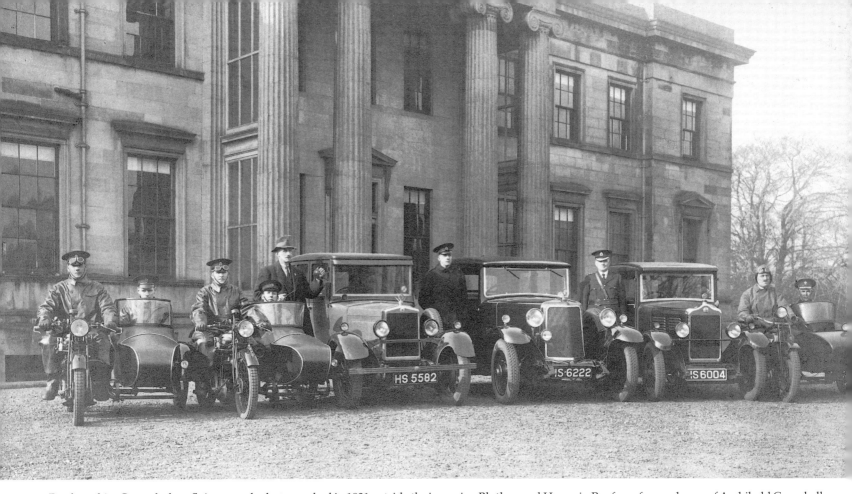

Renfrewshire Constabulary flying squad, photographed in 1931 outside the imposing Blythswood House in Renfrew, former home of Archibald Campbell, Lord Blythswood. Built in 1820, the stately mansion entertained many important guests over the years including Sir Walter Scott in 1827 and the Prince and Princess of Wales (later to become King Edward VII and Queen Alexandra) in 1876. Queen Victoria stayed there in 1888 on the occasion of her visit to open Glasgow's City Chambers, and the future King George V and Queen Mary also stayed at Blythswood on a visit to Glasgow in 1907. The building was demolished in 1935 and Blythswood Industrial Estate, retail stores and Renfrew Golf Club now cover this site, which was originally known as Renfield. The police mobile patrol vehicles were (left to right) 1931 Sunbeam motorcycle combinations HS 6220 and 6221; 1929 Morris Cowley 'Flatnose' HS 5582; 1931 Armstrong–Siddeley HS 6222; 1930 Standard HS 6004; and 1929 BSA motorcycle combination HS 5465. The county constabulary was established in 1840, but in 1857 the Royal Burgh of Renfrew formed its own force and retained its independence until police reorganisation in 1930. In 1967 the Paisley Burgh and Greenock Burgh forces also joined what had become Renfrew & Bute Constabulary in 1949. Later changes saw the huge Strathclyde Police Force assume control in 1975.

The Port Glasgow Motor Co. was founded in 1945 and is still operated by the Pollock family, who also controlled James Pollock & Sons, haulage contractors, whose horse-drawn carts and later motor lorries were a familiar sight in Inverclyde. As Austin agents it was natural that the family should own cars of this make, and this scene from 1950 shows, from the left, Walter Pollock with DHS 310, an Austin 16 of 1947, and James Pollock with CHS 651, an Austin 8 convertible which had served with the War Department during the 1939–45 hostilities but was totally reconditioned, repainted and re-registered in 1946 by the Pollocks. The third car is equally interesting, being one of the first pedal cars to be based on the Austin 7 racing car and known as the 'Pathfinder Special'. These were built from 1949 by former miners at a factory in Bargoed, South Wales, and were the pride and joy of any small boy lucky enough to possess one, in this case Walter Pollock Jnr. It even carried 'pretend' registration number PHS 1. The location is Mirren Shore, near the West Quay, Port Glasgow, looking across the Clyde towards Dunbartonshire.

In addition to those described on page 11, other early motor cars built in the county included the Seetstu and the Ridley, manufactured in Paisley by James McGeoch of Incle Street and George Ridley of George Place. Neither were built in any quantity and both had ceased production by about 1910. Stonefield Trucks started life in Lochfield Road, Paisley, in 1974 before moving to Cumnock, while over in East Renfrewshire James Anderson of Newton Mearns built several 'Anderson Specials' for his own use in motor sport events and trials in the 1920s and 30s. One of these is preserved in Glasgow's Museum of Transport. The best-known car to have been built in Renfrewshire was the widely-acclaimed Hillman Imp, introduced in 1963 and the Rootes Group's answer to the Mini. This view at the Linwood Road factory shows a locally-registered two-door example of the popular wee saloon in 1969, with a Guy Arab double decker of Graham's Bus Service of Hawkhead passing behind en route to Linwood. Also constructed here were the Hillman Hunter, and from 1976 the Avenger, on a site adjacent to where the Pressed Steel Co. had previously built coupé bodies for Volvo. The giant American Chrysler Corporation had acquired control of the Rootes Group, but in 1979 sold the troubled company with its history of industrial relations problems to the French Peugeot–Citroen group which revived the Talbot name at Linwood. The whole complex, including Pressed Steel, closed in May 1981, adding to Scotland's long list of failed motor manufacturers. One of the few reminders of Linwood's car production era left today is the fast-fading sign on the railway bridge at Linwood Toll which reads TALBOT LINWOOD PLANT.

he Station, Bishopton.

A Glasgow-bound train pauses at Bishopton station en route from Gourock in the early 1920s when the line was controlled by the Caledonian Railway Company. The 4-4-0 locomotive is CR No. 721, which was built in 1896 to the design of John F. McIntosh and was the first in the series of the famous 'Dunalastair' class: accordingly it carried this name, which came from the Perthshire estate of the Caledonian Railway chairman. These popular locos achieved wide fame at the time as a result of their fine performances on express trains, and were used on the Clyde Coast services in the post-First World War period. Bishopton station as seen in this view is still recognisable today, although the signal cabin no longer exists on the down platform. **17**

Renfrewshire's first regular motor bus service was provided by the Caledonian Railway Company between Clarkston station and Eaglesham. This was operated in conjunction with its own trains from Glasgow Central to Clarkston and commenced in December 1905 using the Wolseley double decker pictured here. This had been part of an order cancelled by the London Motor Omnibus Co. Ltd. and was hired from the manufacturer for three months – thus it could claim to be the first 'London bus' to operate in Scotland. Over half a century later, former London RT type buses ran with McGill of Barrhead and Cunningham of Paisley, while in the 1980s Routemasters were operated by Clydeside Buses. The Caley Railway ceased this bus service in 1909, but the operation was continued by the Caledonian Automobile Services Ltd. of Glasgow, one of whose vehicles is illustrated below. Additional early bus services in the county were introduced in 1906 by another railway company, the Glasgow & South Western, between Johnstone station, Crosslee and Houston, and also from Johnstone station to Milliken Park and Howwood, but were short-lived ventures.

Eaglesham is an attractive conservation village in East Renfrewshire, and in Victorian and Edwardian times was a popular beauty spot for day excursions from Glasgow. Andrew Jamieson of Eaglesham was one of the local jobmasters who provided horse-drawn transport between the village and the Corporation tram terminus at Cathcart, six miles distant. He was also early to recognise the benefits of motor transport, replacing four of his three-horse brakes with a new Arrol–Johnston charabanc in 1909. Also operating to Eaglesham prior to the First World War was the Caledonian Automobile Service from Clarkston, whose 1910 Halley charabanc, V 1967, is seen here. George Halley of Halley Motors, Yoker, was a director of the CAS. The chassis and engine of V 1967 were built in Yoker (which at that time was still part of Renfrewshire) while the 35-seat bodywork was by John Steel of Wishaw and featured an individual door to each of the seven rows of seats. This was No. 6 in the Caledonian Auto Services fleet and was photographed in Eaglesham with driver John McGuire. The conductor had to work his way precariously along the running boards during the journey in order to collect the fares.

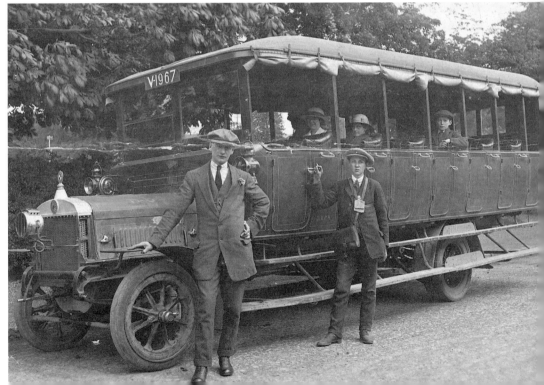

Among several bus operators serving the route between Glasgow, Barrhead and Neilston in the 1920s was the partnership of Robertson & Lennox, based in Bellfield Street, Barrhead. Here Alex Robertson is seen on the step of his new Commer at the Neilston terminus in 1926. The disc showing NB on the front window signified membership of the Neilston & Barrhead Bus Owners' Association, with common fares and interchangeable tickets on other NB buses. Bodywork on this 26-seater was built in London by Hall, Lewis and was a step forward in comfort over the small 14- and 20-seat Beardmores and Reos which also worked the service. Some of the rival owners included Carmichael Bros. of Neilston (who operated Lancias); O'Hara & Sons of George Street, Barrhead, with Oldsmobile charabancs named *Bluebell*, *Daisy*, *Primrose* and *Violet*; William Houston, Spur Inn, Barrhead (Fiat, Reo and Albion); William Wardrop, Muriel Street, Barrhead (GMC, Lancia and Chevrolet); John Hughes of Neilston, who had been a goalkeeper for Celtic FC and operated Reo and Albion vehicles; and Wm. Wright of Lochlibo Crescent, Barrhead (Reo and Lancia). Robertson & Lennox subsequently sold their business to King's Motor Service of Pollokshaws, one of the larger operators on the Neilston route. The pioneer motor bus service between Barrhead and Neilston had been initiated by local baker David Danks of Neilston in 1922 using a converted Ford van.

One of the most lucrative bus services in Scotland served the busy route between Glasgow, Paisley and Johnstone. In the late 1920s two major bus companies competed against the Glasgow Corporation tramway system over the route. One was locally-based Young's Bus Service of Paisley and the other was the Midland Bus Service of Airdrie. In addition, there were as many as 50 smaller operators, most of which were owner/drivers with only one or two buses, all vying with each other for passengers. This photograph, taken in Young's Johnstone garage in Mary Street, shows a line of Northern Counties-bodied Guy Arab double deckers which were purchased in 1946 and used on the main YBS routes from Glasgow to Johnstone, Largs and West Kilbride. Young's Bus Service, with its distinctive orange and cream livery, had grown from owning one single-deck Albion in 1925 to a fleet of 95 double-deck Albions, Daimlers, Guys and Leylands, plus three Bedford and ten Maudslay coaches, all of which were taken over in 1951 when the company was absorbed by Western SMT. Western continued to utilise Young's former operational and maintenance premises at Milliken Park and Mary Street in Johnstone, a small depot in Largs, and also the Gordon Street depot in Paisley of the Paisley & District Omnibus Company, which had been a subsidiary of YBS since 1933 and provided a further 22 Daimler and Guy double deckers when Western took over.

In contrast to the fleet pictured opposite, this view shows a long line of Albions (with a few Leylands at the far end), all of which were owned by Midland Bus Services of Airdrie, a company which from the mid- to late-1920s was a major rival to Young's Bus Service of Paisley. The Midland company was owned by John C. Sword, who may be seen on the extreme right. Sword was a man of vision and a transport entrepreneur and pioneer. Not only did he build up a very successful bus company, with a network of services in many areas of Renfrewshire, Ayrshire and Lanarkshire and long-distance express links from Glasgow to Lancashire and London, he also founded Midland & Scottish Air Ferries in 1932, based at Renfrew Aerodrome. The famous Scottish Air Ambulance services to the Western Isles were also pioneered by John Sword and, moreover, Sword's planes were the first to use the field which later became part of Prestwick Airport. Sword sold his company to the expanding Scottish Motor Traction Co. in 1929, and when Western SMT was formed in 1932 he became the first general manager, a position also occupied by his son William from 1951. The 'model 24' type Albions pictured here were purchased in 1925 to inaugurate Midland's service between Glasgow and Paisley, which was soon extended to Johnstone. They were an assortment of red-liveried 20- and 24-seaters, with similar bodywork by Stewart of Wishaw and Northern Counties of Wigan.

Unmistakably Paisley and unmistakably Albion, this view from 1934 looks towards the George A. Clark town hall and Clark's Mills beyond, while one of the first members of the original fleet of double deckers belonging to locally-owned Young's Bus Service picks up passengers at the Johnstone bus stop, which at that time was on St James Bridge over the River Cart at Paisley Cross. The bus was XS 3322, No. 80 in the YBS fleet and one of twelve Albion Venturers with bodywork by Northern Counties of Wigan delivered to Young's that year. It survived to become part of the Western SMT fleet when that company acquired Young's business in 1951. Also shown is a typical 'setright' return ticket issued by Young's buses.

In 1929, to complement its rail services, the London, Midland & Scottish Railway commenced a bus service in Renfrewshire from Greenock via Gourock and the coast to Wemyss Bay and on to Largs. Another service linked Glasgow with Largs via Renfrew, Bishopton and the Inverclyde towns. The main type of bus used on these services was the Albion 30/60 h.p. single decker, a typical example of which is seen here. The buses were not registered in Renfrewshire but Derbyshire – LMS heartland – and this one was CH 7930 with 32-seat rear-entrance bodywork built by the railway company in its Derby workshops. It was finished in a plum-coloured livery which displayed the railway crest on the side panels. When the giant SMT group of companies was formed in the early 1930s, with a working radius covering most parts of Scotland, LMSR ceased its bus operations which then passed to Western SMT control.

Once well-known among the many independent bus operators in Renfrewshire was the name of Garner, Bridge of Weir. The Garner family originally ran a horse-drawn carriage from Bridge of Weir railway station to Quarrier's Homes, which was replaced by a bus when motors ousted horses. Shortly before the outbreak of the Second World War in 1939, the Royal Ordnance Factory at Bishopton started to expand considerably and Garners won the contract to operate transport services to the factory from all over the county. It was at this time that Garners built their garage in Main Street, Bridge of Weir, on the site of the former livery stables, a project which also involved demolishing a tenement building and Hood & Barr's plumbers' shop. Garner's garage premises are visible to the left of the photograph of FUS 970, a 1948 Croft-bodied Commer which was one of several second-hand purchases in the early 1960s from David MacBrayne, one of whose former Maudslays is also visible in this view. The Commer is departing the village on service to Quarrier's orphan homes.

Contract work was always the mainstay of the business under the able leadership of Miss Dolly Garner. Apart from the ROF work, other contracts were operated for workers at Ferguslie, Anchor and Crosslee Mills and Stoddard's Elderslie carpetfield. Hunterston power station also provided a large amount of custom with Garners buses ferrying workers there from all over Renfrewshire and Lanarkshire in an assortment of over 40 second-hand double deckers, three of which are seen in this picture in the early 1950s. The oldest of this trio of Leylands is GE 5101, in the centre, which had started life running for the Glasgow General Omnibus Co. (forerunner of Central SMT) in 1929. The other two (GWJ 623 and EWJ 294) were formerly with Sheffield Corporation. Garner's also ran single deck service buses on routes between Houston and Johnstone (originally operated by Hutton of Houston), and after the Second World War between Bridge of Weir and Paisley via Georgetown. The company's fortunes declined when the contract work diminished and the business closed in 1968.

Passing the Clyde Rubber Works in French Street, Renfrew in the mid-1950s on a special service to the adjacent Babcock & Wilcox factory is YS 2086, a 1936 Albion Venturer belonging to Paton Bros., one of several purchased second-hand from Glasgow Corporation in 1946. The Patons had started business in the early 1920s operating a bus between Inchinnan and Renfrew, and also between Renfrew Ferry and Paisley in opposition to the Glasgow trams. From its original base in Fulbar Street, Renfrew, the company moved in the late 1920s to a site at the ferry known as Tower Garage after the huge electricity pylon (see pages 38 and 39). Journeys to Glasgow were also operated for a period in the late 1920s when bus services were very much a free-for-all prior to the introduction of the 1930 Road Traffic Act. With the development of Hillington Industrial Estate in the late 1930s, workers' services were introduced to provide a link from both Renfrew and Paisley, while the company's main route between the ferry and Paisley was increased to a three-bus operation with the withdrawal of the Corporation trams in 1957. In addition, services were provided between Paisley, Renfrew and Govan and also for many local schools. In 1979 Paton Bros. sold their business to Western SMT, thus ending over half a century of service with the familiar blue buses in Renfrew and district.

Pictured in Inchinnan Road, Renfrew, at the former West Lodge to Blythswood Estate, is HS 5714, a Leyland Lion LT2 model with Leyland's own bodywork which was delivered in 1930 to Robert and William Ferguson of Victoria Drive, Renfrew. At that time Fergusons' 'Victoria' bus service operated a ten minute frequency between Glasgow, Renfrew and Gourock whereas today there is no link from Renfrew to the Inverclyde towns! The Victoria buses were mainly Albions and Leylands finished in a very attractive deep plum-coloured livery with a gold band. The company moved to new, purpose-built premises at Inchinnan before selling the business to the expanding SMT group in November 1931. Inchinnan depot has since been used by Western SMT, Clydeside Buses, and now Arriva Buses.

Opposite: This advert describes Fergusons' Victoria operation in 1930 and pictures the fleet outside the original Renfrew garage.

VICTORIA SALOON BUS SERVICE . . Glasgow AND Gourock

ROUTE:—LEAVE CARLTON PLACE, GLASGOW; Govan; Princes Docks; Elder Park; Shieldhall New Docks; Renfrew Town Hall and War Memorial; Blythswood Policies; Rivers White and Black Cart; Inchinnan; India Tyre Factory; Bishopton; Hatton Hill; West Ferry (opposite Dumbarton Rock); Langbank; Finlaystone; Parklee; Port-Glasgow Town Hall and War Memorial; Greenock: James Watt Dock, Cathcart Square; Fort Matilda; Battery Park; Cardwell Bay; to Pierhead, Gourock.

THE FINEST BUS RUN IN THE WEST OF SCOTLAND TO THE BEST AND MOST CONVENIENT CLYDE COAST RESORT

Unsurpassed Scenery on the Route . . . View the unrivalled setting of the Clyde from the Hatton Hill, Ben Lomond forming the background

PART OF THE "VICTORIA" FLEET ON THE GLASGOW—GOUROCK ROUTE

FIRST BUSES LEAVE GLASGOW AND GOUROCK AT 6.30 A.M. AND RUN EVERY 10 MINUTES UNTIL MIDNIGHT

100　　VICTORIA BUSES arrive and depart from Pierhead EVERY DAY
Service Augmented during Holiday Week-Ends and Rush Periods　　**100**

R. & W. FERGUSON, VICTORIA GARAGE, RENFREW - 'PHONE: RENFREW 114

Victor Sun Saloon Coaches was the fleet name of Daniel Ferguson of Victoria Garage, Renfrew, who occupied the premises in Victoria Drive which had been the base for Robert and William Ferguson's 'Victoria' bus service prior to their move to new premises at Inchinnan. Daniel's father (also Daniel) was Provost of Renfrew between 1918 and 1924 and had owned a sawmill on the Moorpark site. This utilised a number of Argyll and Halley lorries on local haulage business, which could also be converted to open charabancs for passenger use at weekends. Here two of Ferguson's Albion Victors are seen at the Inchinnan Road junction between the Rivers Black and White Cart. HS 8208 was a 1935 forward-control type with 30-seat coachwork by Cowieson of Glasgow, while HS 7019, dating from 1933, was a normal-control (bonnet type) with rear-entrance 24-seat bodywork built by Cadogan of Perth. At this period the fleet livery was red and grey, but after acquisition by Isaac Barrie of Glasgow during the war years this was changed to green and black. In addition to private hire work a bus was operated on the busy service between Paisley and Renfrew Ferry, and this passed to Cunningham's Bus Service of Paisley in 1953 when 'Victor' ceased trading.

TELEPHONE: RENFREW 2758

DANIEL FERGUSON LTD.

MODERN LUXURY TRAVEL

Motor Coach and Bus Operators Private Hire

VICTOR SUN SALOON COACHES

VICTORIA GARAGE—RENFREW

MANAGER: PETER HAMILTON

Drivers Adam Wade (left) and Jimmy Craig pose with a passenger prior to departing with a group of senior citizens on a day outing from Fulbar Street, Renfrew in the mid-1950s. The coaches were both second-hand purchases owned by Cunningham of Underwood Road, Paisley: JTD 547 was an uncommon 1948 Tilling Stevens with Dutfield coachwork, while EYS 837 was a former Lowland Motorways 1947 Duple-bodied AEC Regal. Cunningham's operated a lot of this type of private charter work, and in addition ran five double deckers on the intensive and competitive local service between Paisley and Renfrew Ferry after Glasgow Corporation withdrew its Paisley area tram services in 1957. Cunningham's sold their business to Western SMT of Kilmarnock in 1979, as did Paton Bros. of Renfrew, who also operated various local services in the area.

In 1932 Glasgow Corporation Transport abandoned the Kilbarchan tram service (which had originally been provided by Paisley District Tramways) and substituted buses on the route. The following year saw a further Paisley tramway withdrawal when GCT ceased running the single-deck service between County Square and Abbotsinch, replacing it with bus service 17. In 1943 these initially separate bus routes were linked to become service 12 from Kilbarchan via Johnstone and Paisley to Abbotsinch, and remained as such until 1955 when the Corporation axed all their bus services outwith the city boundary. The Paisley area routes then passed to Western SMT. This 1950 scene at Houston Square in Johnstone outside the former YWCA building shows a typical example of the type of Corporation bus used on services operated by Elderslie depot. A 115 (FYS 215) was an AEC Regent III, new in 1949 with bodywork by Metro–Cammell of Birmingham, who many years later were to build Glasgow's 'clockwork orange' underground railway coaches. Following closely behind is Glasgow-bound XS 6416, No. 164 in the Young's Bus Service fleet. This was a 1948 Leyland Titan PD2 bodied by

30 Northern Counties of Wigan, and was to be repainted from Young's orange to Western SMT red in 1951 when YBS sold out.

James Smith of Aurs Road was one of a number of bus operators based in Barrhead (see page 19), and from 1927 operated the Paisley to Nitshill service previously run by Joe Arlet of Paisley. Smith sold his business to the Scottish Co-operative Wholesale Society in 1947 at a time when the SCWS was taking an increasing interest in transport companies, although the society continued to operate it under Smith's name and livery. This scene in Paisley shows Crossley GGA 75 leaving the Cotton Street stance for Nitshill. This bus was new in 1948 with bodywork by Roe of Leeds, finished in Smith's dark green and cream colours. Note the in-house advert for 'Waxwing' shoe polish, which was a Co-op product. In 1968 the SCWS sold the Smith operation to Western SMT of Kilmarnock. New Crossley double deckers were relatively uncommon in Scotland but during the early 1960s Graham's Bus Service of Hawkhead operated a few second-hand examples from Barrow Corporation.

Earlier examples of Smith's fleet included these two coaches of the 1930s, since at that time James Smith ran a selection of day and extended tours from Barrhead. Leading is HS 7605, a Leyland Lion of 1934, followed by HS 7112, a Morris of 1933. Both had bodywork built by Duple of Hendon, London.

Today the western end of the M8 motorway to Edinburgh starts near Langbank and runs attractively along the southern shore of the River Clyde with views across to Dumbarton and its famous landmark rock and castle. However, before the welcome construction of the M8 – aimed to alleviate increasing congestion on this busy corridor – traffic used what is now the A8. This scene from 1957 shows the old road climbing the Hatton Brae from West Ferry, with a then new Western SMT coach featuring the unusual combination of Bristol chassis and Alexander bodywork. Numbered 1276 in the fleet, this was one of nineteen similar dual-purpose vehicles and was based at the now-closed Greenock depot at Inchgreen. When this photograph was taken, Western SMT operated a basic fifteen minute frequency between Glasgow, Renfrew, Bishopton, Langbank, Port Glasgow, Greenock and Gourock, with an hourly extension via the coast to Largs. These services ceased operating many years ago, and today one cannot travel by bus direct from Renfrew to the Inverclyde towns or Largs.

Repair works on the bridge and roadway over the River White Cart at Inchinnan Road, Renfrew seem to be a never-ending affair. The red warning sign for road works is prominent in this scene from March 1965, although the 'SLOW' sign has gone from the bridge today. A Western SMT Albion Lowlander crosses on route 23 from Glasgow to Gourock, followed by a Bedford van owned by the United Co-operative Bakery Society. The bus was VCS 434, numbered 1880, and was one of a large fleet of this type, some of which were bodied by Northern Counties of Wigan, while others, such as the 1963 example seen here, were built by Alexander of Falkirk. This one was based with several others at Western's nearby Inchinnan depot. The bascule bridge, familiarly but wrongly referred to by most local folk for many years as the 'swing bridge', replaced the previous structure in 1923 and is now the only surviving rolling lift bridge in Scotland.

Paddle wheels passing Gourock in late Victorian times, seen from the approximate site of today's information kiosk in Kempock Place. This photograph was taken by W. Morris Robertson looking towards the pier head – or quay head as it was then known – and the houses of Kilcreggan across the Clyde on the north bank. Even then it was a rather untidy area, with Robertson's photographic premises prominent on the left and a shooting range on the shore. Steaming away from the pier is PS *Elaine*, whose open decks are heavily laden with day trippers. *Elaine* was built at Duncan's yard in Port Glasgow in 1867 and her original owners were Graham, Brymner & Co., who employed her on the sailing between Glasgow and Millport. This scene, however, shows her in service with Captain William Buchanan for whom she plied for about twenty years, mainly on river routes such as Broomielaw–Rothesay and Broomielaw–Garelochhead.

During construction of the Cunard White Star liner *Queen Mary* at John Brown's Clydebank yard, a huge number of spectators would gather to watch progress from the opposite shore of the Clyde where the best views could be obtained – usually from Garnieland Farm on the Inchinnan side of the River Cart and Blythswood Estate on the Renfrew side. This view shows a typical group of assorted onlookers who have braved the muddy conditions on foot, by bicycle and motorbike to admire what was then the world's largest vessel. The name of the cloth-capped motorcyclist is not known, but his Glasgow-registered bike, US 1849, was a 1933 AJS. Work on hull No. 534 was halted and 3,000 shipyard workers were laid off in 1931 when Cunard faced financial collapse. However, building recommenced in 1934 once Cunard had agreed terms with the government for additional funding. The vessel was launched and named *Queen Mary* in 1934, and her maiden voyage took place in 1936. She continued to carry mainly prosperous clients across the Atlantic until 1967, when she was sold to become a hotel and conference centre at Long Beach, California.

Renfrewshire boasted three electric tramway operators in the first quarter of the twentieth century. The district now known as Inverclyde was served by the Greenock & Port Glasgow Tramways Co., while the area around Paisley, Johnstone, Renfrew and Barrhead was the province of Paisley District Tramways Co. until 1923, when the company was acquired by Glasgow Corporation Tramways. GCT was the other tramway operator in the county since some of its services overlapped the city boundary into Renfrewshire – for instance to Paisley, Renfrew, Thornliebank, Merrylee, Giffnock and Clarkston. This scene probably dates from the summer of 1906, shortly after the Paisley company opened the Kilbarchan extension of its line to Johnstone – and was almost certainly taken on a Sunday as everyone is dressed in their best. At that time Kilbarchan tramway terminus was outside the Trust Inn, visible on the left in Low Barholm, but in 1913 the line was extended further into the village to High Barholm. The tramcar in this picture is No. 38, one of the original red and white liveried open-top Paisley cars built by the British Electric Car Co. of Trafford Park, Manchester, on Brush trucks and delivered for the opening of the electric tramway in 1904. The trams provided an excellent means of mobile advertising for local firms and space on this one was taken up by Cairns' Marmalade. This was manufactured in Paisley by Alexander Cairns & Sons at St George preserve works in Clark Street – a rival at that time to Robertson's on the other side of the town. Also illustrated is a ha'penny tram ticket from Edwardian times which shows each 'fare station' on the nine-mile route from Renfrew Ferry to Kilbarchan.

The Paisley District Tramways Co. stabled its cars at three depots throughout the system – Elderslie, Renfrew (closed 1936) and a small site at Barrhead. Only Elderslie depot remained operational under Glasgow Corporation Transport control through to the end of the Paisley area tram services in 1957. It also served as a bus garage for the GCT local services. This view from the adjacent railway embankment looking east towards Linwood Toll shows three cars making their way back to the depot after morning peak services on 6 August 1953. Standard car 281 dating from 1909 is on the short spur line leading to the depot 'lyes', where the covered lines of trams were housed. Car 6 waits its turn; it was one of five lightweight experimental cars built during the Second World War by Glasgow Corporation. All were based at Elderslie and as their reliability was poor they were used mainly on local peak hour duties. Approaching is one of the popular Coronation cars (so-called since this type arrived at the time of the accession to the throne of King George VI and Queen Elizabeth in 1937). Also visible are two former Young's Bus Service Daimlers, working from Glasgow to Johnstone for Western SMT. Immediately behind the conductor directing traffic is the two-storey depot 'bothy' where the crews (green staff) and maintenance fitters (black squad) enjoyed their tea breaks.

Renfrew Ferry was the terminus for busy Glasgow Corporation tram service 28 which ran latterly from Glenfield through Paisley and Renfrew. In the period between 1934 and 1943 it was possible to enjoy Britain's longest tram journey from Renfrew Ferry all the way to Barrhead, through Glasgow and north to Maryhill and Milngavie – 23 miles for twopence ha'penny. This mid-1950s photograph by transport enthusiast Jim Thomson – who as a boy crossed the ferry by bike on photographic expeditions from his home in Blawarthill – was taken on a quiet morning after a shower of rain and shows car 77 reflected as it departs for Elderslie. No. 260, in the foreground, has just arrived from Glenfield and has its destination screen changed ready for its next journey to Lochfield Road, a short working which was operated alternately with Glenfield runs. Visible on the north side of the river at Yoker are the chimneys of the now-demolished Clyde Valley power station, while behind Coia's cafe is the huge electricity pylon which gave its name to Paton's Tower Garage, where some of that company's buses may be seen.

Renfrew Ferry was not only the terminus for Glasgow Corporation tram service 28, but also for the peak hour special workings on bus service 12 to Kilbarchan. A workman sprints to catch Coronation car 1282 (now preserved at Crich National Tramway Museum in Derbyshire) as it departs for Lochfield Road, while AEC Regent A110 (FYS 210) leaves London Street for Kilbarchan. Also visible in this animated scene from 1954 is the queue of assorted vehicles waiting to cross the ferry, while a 1939 Austin car (DGB 475) approaches the camera. A former Young's Bus Service Albion Venturer (XS 4132) in Western SMT colours waits at the Paisley bus stop, while across the street one of Paton's blue double deckers is parked in their Tower Garage yard. Originally the tram terminus was located outside the Ferry Inn, but was curtailed to London Street at Coia's cafe to ease the congestion caused by traffic queuing for the ferry.

The picture on the front cover shows the fondly-remembered chain ferry at Renfrew, while this scene from the same period in the early 1950s shows the view from the upper deck of the ferry as it arrives at the Renfrew shore. At this time there was huge demand for the ferry by both motor and pedestrian traffic, since industry on both sides of the river was booming (e.g. Babcock's; Simon's; Lobnitz; and India Tyres on the Renfrew side, and Albion Motors; Bull's; Drysdale's; Yarrow's; and John Brown's on the north side, to name but a few). This is confirmed by the long but orderly queue of workers seen here returning home. Two Clyde Navigation Trust employees prepare to open the gates at the top of the ramp for motor vehicles leaving the ferry, while a line of traffic waits to cross to Yoker. A big Austin Princess limousine heads the queue of assorted cars, which after a gap outside Coia's cafe – to avoid jamming London Street junction and the tram terminus – continues again beyond the waiting tram and extends towards Meadowside Street.

Road traffic accidents are by no means a modern phenomenon. This one took place near Mearnskirk in 1924 when the driver of the Leyland lorry ended up with his wagon well and truly in the ditch and the tipper body totally removed, having tried to avoid a motor car. Providing assistance is the Ford road rescue service operated by Andersons of Newton Mearns. The Leyland was HS 1138, a 35/40 h.p. model which had been new in March 1919 to Wallace & Co., Netherplace, Newton Mearns, members of the Calico Printers' Association. This was an old-established firm of cloth bleachers, dyers and finishers which was one of the main employers in the Mearns area. In 1980 the firm closed, which was a double blow to the local community since Andersons Garage shut in the same year. However, six years later the Netherplace factory reopened and now trades as Coats Barbour. Recently it provided threads for use in costumes for the 2002 film *Harry Potter and the Chamber of Secrets*.

As explained on page 8, the old Renfrewshire county boundary extended to the north side of the Clyde, and the Albion motor works at Scotstoun fell within it. Renfrewshire companies remained faithful to sturdy Albion trucks and buses over the years (the Albion slogan was 'Sure as the Sunrise'), and the pictures on this double page spread feature some local firms which chose the popular breed. This one shows an Albion CX1 model which went to Babcock & Wilcox, the Renfrew-based engineering company (whose 'Steam' logo may be seen on the cab door) in 1947. Babcock's earliest motor lorries had been HS 421 and 610, two Karrier 20 h.p. 2½ tonners, delivered in 1912.

D. & J. Eadie, the Johnstone potato merchants, painted their Albions in a smart green livery and FHS 49 was a Chieftain which was new in 1951. Another link with Renfrewshire common to both this Albion and the one belonging to Babcock's is that each was shod with Red Line tyres. These were made by India of Inchinnan at their fine 1930 factory, which has been recently restored and extended and which stands on the site where airships R33 and R34 had been built.

EHS 979 was an Albion FT3 six-cylinder petrol-engined tipper, and is seen shortly after delivery in 1951 outside the office door at Stoddard's carpet factory in Glenpatrick Road, Elderslie. This was known locally as 'the carpetfield' and closed completely in 2003, ending an association going back as far as the 1860s when Arthur Stoddard began carpet manufacture here.

Haulage contractors J. & M. Taylor of Wallace Street, Paisley were well-known for their lorry fleet but are perhaps less remembered for their small fleet of mechanical shovels, which were particularly popular before the introduction of JCBs. EXS 869F was typical of these vehicles and was a Chaseside SL 704 model with six-cylinder Ford engine, painted in a plain yellow livery as opposed to Taylor's green and red lorries. It is seen here shortly after delivery in February 1968, working on hire at the premises of Saunders & Connor, sanitary engineers and ironfounders in Muriel Street, Barrhead (the council houses just visible at the upper right are in Commercial Road). The company specialised in the manufacture of cast iron baths and cisterns, and in this view the mechanical shovel is about to carry a load of foundry coke to feed the factory furnace. Behind the Chaseside is a pile of scrap iron which would be melted down to make the baths. Saunders & Connor later became part of Allied Ironfounders, but the Barrhead business closed in the 1980s.

In addition to their passenger transport operations, the Young family of Paisley branched into road haulage in the mid-1930s when they started Young's Express Deliveries having acquired the existing lorry fleet operated by Scottish Express Deliveries in Pollokshaws Road, Glasgow. A move was made around 1938 to an operating base in Scotland Street, and then in 1940 to Portman Street near Paisley Road Toll, which remained the main Scottish depot until nationalisation in 1949. Other YED depots were located at Abington, Edinburgh, Inverness, Kirkcaldy, Oban, Birmingham, Manchester and London, and their green and red liveried lorries (ultimately 275 at time of nationalisation) were a familiar sight throughout the UK in the 1930s and 40s. The company head office, however, had always shared the address of Young's Bus Service at 4 Gordon Street, Paisley. Much of the major maintenance work on the fleet was carried out under the eye of Gordon Young at the Mary Street depot in Johnstone, home of Young's bus fleet. Day-to-day repairs were handled at individual depots. Other family members looking after the business were Ian and Robin Young at the Glasgow base. Some of the bodywork on the lorry fleet was constructed by Young's own coachbuilding department in Johnstone, including a number of the big Scammells which were amongst the final wagons in the fleet prior to British Road Services operation. Just after the Second World War, when YED was still under control of the Ministry of War Transport, this fleet of ERF wagons and a single Foden worked for several months in Germany delivering salt. The code on the cabs signifies that the lorries operated under Foreign Service Unit No. 2 with their respective individual numbers. The newest of these vehicles was XS 5636, an ERF of 1945, while most of the others dated from 1936 and were acquired by YED from a Lancashire contractor during wartime. Foden YJ 6112 had been new in 1938 and originally ran with Easson of Dundee.

Aircraft have wheels as well as wings and have played an important part in the economy of Renfrewshire, with vast numbers of passengers passing through Glasgow Airport at Abbotsinch (and previously Renfrew Airport until 1966). Renfrew Aerodrome was operational as far back as 1914 and later saw particularly rapid development after the end of the Second World War in 1945. For many years it was the Scottish headquarters of British European Airways, and this scene from 1954 shows a number of BEA aircraft at Renfrew, with the Moorpark area of the town in the background. To the left, beyond the airport, may be seen the paintworks which was situated at the junction of Cockels Loan and Sandy Road. Today a memorial cairn stands at the corner of Sandy Road and Newmains Road as a tribute to the men and women of the Scottish Air Ambulance Service.

Connecting buses for flights from Renfrew Airport were originally operated in the 1930s and 40s by Scottish Airways using their own Bedford coaches. In later years, Lowland Motorways of Glasgow (trading as Greyhound Coaches) obtained the contract and ran from the air terminal in St Enoch Square to the airport. In contrast to the strict regulations in force today, airport rules were formerly considerably more lax, as this scene from the late 1950s verifies with Lowland coaches delivering passengers direct to the plane. Alongside the BEA Vickers Viscount is OGG 273, an Albion Victor new in 1955 with coachwork of rather severe appearance by Strachans of Acton.

Those who remember Renfrew Airport will recall its modernistic architecture, which incorporated a significant archway over the main entrance to the terminal building. This was situated at the very top of Newmains Road and remained intact for several years after the airport transferred to its present site at Abbotsinch in May 1966. The vehicles visible in this 1956 view are LYN 439, a London-registered 1951 Hillman Minx saloon, and Lowland Motorways JGE 621, a Duple-bodied Bedford SB coach of 1951 providing the airport link to Glasgow. Lowland sold out to SMT (Scottish Omnibuses Ltd.) of Edinburgh in 1958, which passed the Renfrew Airport connecting services to Western SMT, who operated these from their depot at Inchinnan and continued to do so after the airport moved to Abbotsinch in 1966.

The name McKelvie is usually associated with the fleet of lorries owned by the former haulage company based in Barrhead. Less well-known is the fact that during the 1940s and 50s McKelvie's also operated coaches. EHS 424 of 1950 had been a member of the company's continental coach fleet (tours were operated to the French and Italian Rivieras), but after that side of the business closed some of the former passenger vehicles were converted to carry lorry bodies, including this Albion Valiant, seen here at the loading bay in the Paisley depot in Clark Street. McKelvie's had started business during the horse-drawn era in the early twentieth century and one of their original contracts was carrying sanitary ware for Shanks of Barrhead.